Resurrection of Your Inner Hero

Rendering Passivity Obsolete

Sidekick

JIM SNYDER

WESTBOW PRESS
A DIVISION OF THOMAS NELSON
& ZONDERVAN

WestBow Press books may be ordered through booksellers or by contacting:

WestBow Press
A Division of Thomas Nelson & Zondervan
1663 Liberty Drive
Bloomington, IN 47403
www.westbowpress.com
1 (866) 928-1240

Cover Photo by: Vernon Photography

ISBN: 978-1-4908-5828-9 (sc)

Library of Congress Control Number: 2014919302

Printed in the United States of America.

WestBow Press rev. date: 11/06/2014

Introduction

I'm glad you have decided to take your journey towards freedom from passivity to the next level by doing the introspective work found within this guide. These questions are designed to get you to identify areas where God wants you to push in.

Read the corresponding chapter, then spend some time pushing into the questions with God. Don't skip chapters or questions because they're difficult. They're designed to build upon one another and get you digging within yourself. Take your time. This is a marathon not a sprint.

First, know that there are no right or wrong answers. Second, the more truthful and open you are with your answers, the more God can help and make changes within you. Third, this is your guide and not your report card. You do not need or have to share it with anyone. Hide it if you have to.

chapter one

What is Passivity?

No man ever wants to admit he's passive. Some may not know what being passive may look like in their lives. We all know that something has been lost in how we function; identifying what was lost is one of the first steps to finding a way to get it back.

How do you identify with Tim in his situation?

Do you feel like there is something "more" you can be?

Can you identify what that "more" is?

What's holding you back?

Passivity is not a black or white, all or none, problem, it is more of a variety of grays or different shades of gray, but if left unchecked passivity can enter into places or areas of strength. Passivity had become like a virus in my life, invading various aspects and areas without ceasing. The more problems came up in life, the more passive I would become.

How extensive has passivity become in your life?

What areas of your life has passivity taken control of?

Have you seen passivity come into places of your strength?

What did that look like?

From the book:

> The same metaphor applies as you learn to learn to crawl towards engaging in the areas my passivity was residing before learning to walk. Once you have the crawling lesson down, you graduate to learning how to walk in that particular area of engaging and ridding yourself further of passivity in that area. With each step, you gain more and more confidence in your abilities until you could turn the walking strides into short sprints and ultimately on your way to running long distances.

What are some areas in your life where you're expecting yourself to be a marathon runner but really you're belly surfing?

What emotions come to mind when you hear that fear is the root of passivity?

Do you act like you don't hear God? Or choose not to "hear" what He says?

Jim Snyder

What has He been telling you that you don't want to do?

chapter two

History of Passivity

The Bible holds many examples of people who found the courage to re-engage. John Eldredge says, "The Bible is not a book of exceptional people doing ordinary things, but ordinary people doing exceptional things." We all relate to the Bible stories in one way or another, finding our place in the ultimate story is essential.

Which person in the Bible do you most identify with? Why?

How is your story the same as that person's?

How is your story different from that person's?

Which person in the Bible do you wish your story was more like? Why?

From the book:

> It becomes apparent that no matter how old you are or how far along in your journey you are, you still can pursue the right way to overcome the fear associated with passivity. Even the man after God's heart (David) went passive. It gives us hope that we can be in God's will despite the occasions when our passivity rears its ugly head. The stress and worry that come from leadership—both business and familial—can be conquered through Christ. There is redemption that can occur when we get out of our passivity as Peter did and we can be used for God's greater purpose.

What stands in the way from you having that life?

How can you take your first baby step towards that life today?

chapter three

My Own Worst Enemy

It is amazing to see the tools Satan and his emissaries use against us in order to keep us under his influence. The use of guilt or perceived guilt can keep us looking backwards into our past rather than looking forward into our future. Being stuck in those lies the enemy tells us keeps us from moving towards God and what He has for us. The following questions will help you identify where Satan is holding you under his thumb. Exposure is the key to breakthrough.

What regrets do you rehearse a different ending to?

What stirs within you when you think about those rehearsals?

What woulda, coulda, and shouldas lie in your regrets?

What regrets have you asked God for forgiveness for?

Which regrets would you like to be free of right now?

What is between you and freedom for that regret?

What would you replace your regret with?

Which tenses (past, present, and future) are you focusing your attention?

Who is affected by your passivity?

From the book:

> Guilt, shame, and condemnation aren't from God. They're tools of Satan and allowing them to be strongholds in your life give him control over you. The Bible clearly states in Ephesians 4:27 "… do not give the devil a foothold." Pastor James said, "The only people invited to a pity party are you and Satan." Most of us do not realize how much our passivity can rob us from our joy in life. Satan wants to keep us under his control and not fulfilling our calling or to be joyful.
>
> Satan uses guilt, shame and condemnation to keep us from success and gaining strength or momentum. He fears we'll become the men God wants us to be meaning we'd be living in joy rather than under his oppression.

What do you feel guilty about?

Who do you feel judged by?

What is God convicting you of?

What guilt is Satan using to make you feel shameful?

What names does Satan use to try and define you?

What names does God call you to combat Satan?

What punishment or condemnation do you feel you have to endure for your passivity?

chapter four

The Haunting Wounds

Our personality and the way we relate to others all seem to stem from the hidden wounds of our youth. This chapter may need to be gone over multiple times as new wounds and layers of wounds are exposed. Remember that Satan is always trying to get you to react out of your wounds rather than your true heart. Take this section slow and really push into it with God. Healing is just around the corner and is the first step to reigniting your inner hero.

From the book:

> A wound is an area in our lives that is painful when talked about and can cause us to react in a manner different from our normal or intended behavior. These wounds have been inflicted at the hands of fathers, mothers, siblings, friends, teachers, or anyone you trusted. Some of the wounds were intentional by the person but most often the wound has been unintentionally passed down through their wounds. All wounds are influenced by Satan. Most of the wounds come early in life when we are more susceptible and have more trust in others. As we get older, the wounds have to be more complicated because we trust less. It's why we often wish for the naïveté of youth.

Figure 4.1 (image courtesy of Chris Herndon)

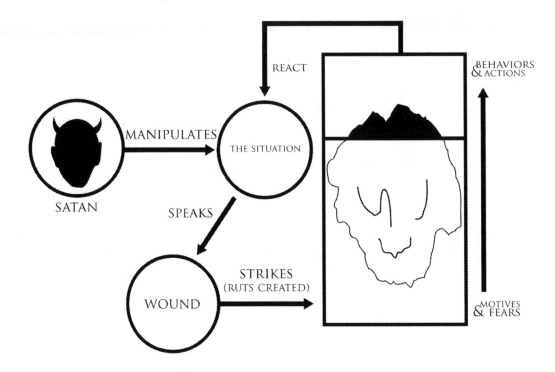

What wound or incident caused you not to trust your parents?

What wound or incident caused you not to trust women?

What wound or incident caused you not to trust other men?

Who do you have in your life that you can truly trust?

What other wounds do you have related to passivity?

What situations do you recall it coming out in?

What motive was used to influence your behavior?

Have you asked God to heal that wound? If not, do so now. If so, how did He heal it?

Defensiveness

At one point in time or another, we have all been backed into a corner whether physically, emotional, or intellectually. These wounds and the feelings of guilt, shame, and condemnation cause us to take a defensive posture. Use these next questions to help guide you through how you react.

From the book:

> The moment we become defensive, we lose our authority and power, but more importantly we lose our capacity for grace, creativity, and ability to hear from God in the moment. In our defensiveness we close most of the available options and reveal our deep fear of inadequacy. We miss the opportunity to guide and direct our families. We also lose the opportunity to teach others how to treat us.

When do you feel cornered?

How do you react when cornered?

When was the last time you felt defensive?

What was the outcome?

What would have been another way to respond?

Where did pride enter in?

From the book:

> The most important and effective tool ever to mitigate defensiveness is regular love and affirmation of men you respect and trust. There is no substitute, and in the instant you start to feel cornered, if you can refocus on the knowledge of being loved and accepted, you can withstand far more, and be a better conduit of grace.

Who are the men you can trust?

Can you "emotionally vomit" on them?

What is your definition of winning the Argument?

What would "winning" look like for Jesus?

Do you feel abused by your spouse?

What steps can you take to eliminate the abuse?

chapter six

Overwhelmed Feeling

At some point in time we all get overwhelmed. This is especially true when we start playing out scenarios in our mind, consuming our working memory. Being overwhelmed can present itself in many different behaviors. None are really our true nature nor shows the true hero within each of us. Spend some time thinking about the various scenarios and possible fantasies that you are playing out in your mind and what they might be prohibiting you from accomplishing.

Have you ever been called lazy?

When do you feel overwhelmed?

What tasks make you feel overwhelmed just mentioning them?

What scenarios are running through your mind now?

What emotions are involved?

From the book:

> Satan manipulates the situation to trigger you into following the emotionally-driven scenarios. The more emotions you spend in the scenarios, the less effective you are in dealing with the immediate situation. Usually, more emotion is spent analyzing the options than is actually used on the initial situation. It's a waste of emotional energy.

What are the negative outcomes in these scenarios?

What are the positive outcomes in these scenarios?

How many levels do your scenarios play out?

What are the unrealistic fantasies you play out in your scenarios?

How close to reality do your fantasies get?

What do you fill up your working memory with?

What categories can you come up with to help manage your life?

Risk: Not the Board Game

One major profound affect of passivity is choosing not to risk getting involved or taking chances. As we've learned in chapter one, God wants us to engage and take risks. Sometimes this lack of risking can appear as patience or procrastination but the truth is that we fear risking. We come up with elaborate excuses to cover up this fear. Rather than making an excuse not to do this chapter, explore where you lack engaging and risking.

Where do you feel that you are a risk taker?

What risks did you take as a youth?

Were they necessary?

Where are you risking nowadays?

What compromises are you making not to risk?

What do you do when it comes to risky decisions?

From the book:

> Often times we mask our passivity in patience by allowing fear to control whether to act in a situation or not. We pawn off our waiting until the situation resolves itself and then we call it "patience."

Have you been told you were a patient man?

Do people come to you for wisdom because of your patience?

Have you ever masked your passivity with patience? When?

Who taught you patience?

Did he or she also teach you passivity?

What percentage of your day are you passive versus actively engaged?

From the book:

> Many people feel that procrastination is just plain laziness and sometimes that is true. However, more often people are willing to take on the task required of them but fear causes them to not engage.

What do you procrastinate doing?

Do you feel that there needs to be an external motivator to get you to stop procrastinating?

What greatness did God build you for?

"Excuses are like armpits, everybody has them and they all stink" – Anonymous
Do you find yourself coming up with excuses not to engage?

What has been your most elaborate excuse not to engage?

What is your "go to" excuse?

From the book:

> When we chose not to engage and it affects someone else, it's selfishness. It doesn't matter if the other person is a friend, spouse, child, parent, co-worker, or stranger. Our selfishness hurts the other person, inflicts a wound, or builds a wall between us. We lose opportunities to build trust, fight for, or minister to others when we choose our own selfishness.

When was the last time someone else asked something of you and you came up with an excuse out of selfishness?

When's the last time you told someone you'd pray for them and didn't?

What has God asked you to do lately that you haven't done?

What excuses do you make out of lack of resources?

Where can you follow through when resources became available?

What excuse do you come up with when you may not have the right skill set?

From the book:

> Fear of situations or fear of being out of control are common excuses not to engage. God calls us to face our fears rather than letting them control us, for the Spirit God gave us does not make us timid, but gives us power, love and self-discipline (2 Timothy 1:7).

How does fear stop you from engaging?

What are you missing out on because of your excuses?

Who are you hurting with your excuses?

What questions can you answer with, "Why Not"?

What are some small activities that you can participate in that is outside your comfort level?

What small areas in your family are you engaging in risk?

How engrossed do you get in taking things on?

What areas of passivity can you be fully engrossed in overcoming?

If you were to engage more in your walk with God, what other areas would come into alignment?

What areas do you struggle dealing with? Why?

What responsibilities do you take on that you shouldn't be?

What fears creep in on you when you don't want to do something?

What "Can of Worms" has God been asking you to open?

chapter eight

Confidence: Building Blocks

We all need confidence if we are going to risk and continue to engage. The problem tends to be that the enemy doesn't want us gaining momentum because confidence instills confidence. The enemy is quick to point out our failures and even quicker to diminish our successes. Challenge yourself with these questions and expose where the enemy is at work.

Since starting the book and engaging, where are you seeing some successes?

How does it feel?

Where are you getting resistance?

Are you getting feedback? And what type is it?

What areas is God upping the ante in?

From the book:

The List

Write down the largest areas where you have influence or are influenced by. Things like God, your spouse, your family, your job, your church or community, your ministry, and your personal life. Take a new notebook and divide it so each area gets the same number of sheets of paper. At the top of the first page of each section, write the subject. Also pick a new writing utensil for this project. Using your writing utensil and journal only for The List will have special meaning later on.

How did it go creating your own List?

Anything you would add to the List?

How does it make you feel to hear that God wants to be your cheerleader?

chapter nine

Taking Things On

One of the toughest parts about overcoming our passivity is confrontation. This confrontation can be towards someone, a situation, or yourself. Figuring our why you don't confront and overcoming it is going to be key to engaging. Use the following questions to pursue your heart's need to confront.

Does confrontation give you anxiety?

From the book:

> Men caught in passivity will more often be a peacekeeper, rather than a peacemaker, of any confrontation, taking on responsibilities and emotional baggage in order to maintain homeostasis or balance within our world. The difference between peacekeeper and peacemaker is where the responsibility and confrontation lies. A peacekeeper takes on all the blame and responsibility as to avoid confrontation. A peacemaker confronts the parties involved and distributes the responsibility accordingly, taking on only what he is responsible for. This doesn't mean that he can delegate all the responsibility to others, just the portions that are not his to take on. In Matthew 5:9, God gives peacemakers a high title. He calls them sons of God. It's easy to take on others' tasks or job functions in order to escape the confrontation with that person but that is not a viable solution.

When do you find yourself the "Peacekeeper" rather than the "Peacemaker"?

What emotional baggage do you take on from being a Peacekeeper?

What goes through your mind when you have to confront someone?

What wound makes you want to avoid confrontation?

Who is the hardest person or group to confront? Why?

Are you worried about how others will perceive you if you confront them? If so, why?

What small areas can you begin to confront people with love?

When do you feel emasculated?

What is your reaction to the emasculated feelings?

From the book:

> Sometimes men who feel emasculated accept the blame, go silent and pout but seek out alternative ways to retaliate. To them retaliation seems justified because they weren't able to rebuttal the conversation the way they felt should have happened. It's a way to punish the other person for making the passive men feel weak. Unfortunately, retaliation is detrimental to relationships, usually backfires, and often causes more grief than pleasure.

What does your passive aggressiveness look like?

What areas are you being passive aggressive in right now?

What are the consequences of your passive aggressiveness?

What are you reaping from it? Is it really working for you or against you?

What actions do you need to take responsibility for?

chapter ten

Anger

Anger is often a destructive way of masking passivity. We all get frustrated from time to time but when we blow up with anger it can have devastating results. Even if you do not overtly struggle with anger, work through these questions to help find your triggers.

Do you struggle with anger? If so, what type?

Do you get angry when you lose control of a situation?

Who is usually the recipient of your anger?

Do you bully?

Have you ever beaten yourself up or put yourself down?

Have you ever gotten angry for something you forgot?

Who has gotten angry with you for forgetting to do something?

Who does your anger affect the most?

From the book:

> Most people who get angry claim that rather than building up, it's a zero to 100 percent in an instant. But that is not really the truth; there are numerous physiological responses that occur prior to the person getting angry but he or she doesn't recognize them because most emotions are shut down.

What are your physical signs of agitation?

What age do you feel when your anger wells up?

What event happened at that age that may have wounded you?

chapter eleven

Addictions

I have yet to meet a man who did not have a vice or some way of checking out. Checking out can be okay, but when abused or used frequently, this can enable your passivity to take over and for you not to be engaged. Addictions can become more than just a way of escaping; they can become a way of life. Use these questions to help identify your checkout mechanisms and their effects on the people in your life.

How often do you find yourself checking out?

What do you turn to when you need to checkout?

Do you consider your checkout an addiction or a vice?

If it's an addiction, what is one way you can step away from that addiction today?

Do you checkout as an excuse or is it to squash a desire?

What are you trying to avoid?

Is there a correlation to your passivity and your checkout mechanism?

How can you modify your checking out to reduce it?

What wound causes you to desire to checkout?

chapter twelve

The Women In Our Lives

This chapter is the longest in the book because women are where we go passive the most. If it wasn't for the women in our lives, most of our passivity wouldn't get exposed and subsequently we would not face it. Women tend to be complicated creatures as they embody the mysteries of God. How we react to them through our passivity can bring them life or death as well as us. Use the following questions to help you reveal where you are going passive and how you can overcome it.

What women do you have influence over?

What are some of the defining moments in your masculinity as it relates to women?

What messages did you learn from these moments?

Jim Snyder

When growing up, who was in charge of the family?

How did your mother treat your heart?

Do you seek out relationships that lend themselves to your passivity?

What areas of your life have you purposely or have manipulated someone else, especially your wife, to do a task that you could have done?

What words, especially from a woman in your life, destroy or tear you to pieces?

Are these words abusive?

Do you struggle expressing how you feel for fear of abuse?

Do you allow or tolerate the little stuff?

From the book:

> Men need tools and a framework to maintain healthy relationship. These tools and framework come from our parents, and specifically our fathers. Think for a minute about the kind of emotional tools your father gave you… If your answer is that he goes passive and retreats, then you may have a critical piece in the puzzle for your own passivity.

What emotional tools did your father equip you with?

How did/does your father handle these things?

Have you ever been referred to as a "nice guy"?

When's the last time you felt like you were being the dutiful husband but longed for some adventure?

When was the last time you manipulated a situation in order to escape from fear?

What excuses do you use to manipulate yourself out of a fearful situation?

From the book:

> Passivity tends to lead to fight or flight mode. It's this adrenaline that gives people super-human strength to lift cars off of their children. Unfortunately it has a downside too of tunnel vision and the inability to focus on more than one thing.
>
> In passivity, that single focus is self-preservation. You perceive danger that may not be real but your reaction to it is. Focusing on self-preservation, you miss great impact your selfish passivity has on others. You're too caught in your own fears to have a genuine concern or compassion for others.

When do you become selfish or self-centered?

How do you recognize your own selfishness or self-centeredness?

Has your wife been sexually abused in her past?

Who is in charge or leads your marriage?

Does your wife want a Biblical marriage?

Are you willing to fight for a Biblical marriage? Even if she initially resists?

What are some small areas or tasks that you can engage in taking over from her?

Does your wife recognize what is missing or not happening in you?

What would it take to get your wife to come alongside you in overcoming your passivity?

What standards or expectations do you feel you are being held to by your wife?

Where and when does your wife encourage you the most? The least?

What areas of your life make you think, "If you engage, she'll come on board?"

What areas do you wish she would encourage you more?

When you look at others' relationships, where do you see the right encouragement and what does it look like?

Does your wife use statements to communicate with you or questions?

Which do you prefer?

What questions does your wife ask you with regards to how she is feeling?

From the book:

> Men in general struggle with knowing how to relate emotionally to other people but the passive man has a harder time relating… The problem stems from the fight or flight mode where you only take into consideration your own thoughts and feelings, especially when the situation involves stress or anxiety. Rather than considering others, you will try to get out of the uncomfortable situation as quickly as possible.

What wounds have you caused or inflicted by being emotionally distant?

What can you do to remedy it?

When have you left your wife emotionally abandoned?

What fears enter into your mind when you think about your wife's emotions?

How do you recognize your wife's emotions?

Do you give your wife ample amounts of time to express her emotions?

From the book:

> Women are sexually aroused by their husband's engagement and conversely do not desire intimacy with their husband when he is passive.

How would you characterize your sex life?

When do you get the most sexual intimacy?

What do you do to "earn" sex?

What could you do to help her?

What fears and anxieties run through your head when I ask you to tell her to let you fail or fall?

chapter thirteen

Putting An End to the Curse

Whether you want to believe it or not, you were called to be a leader. This statement is especially true if you are a father. We are called to lead and teach our families, but sometimes our passivity gets in the way. While we may not have it all figured out, we have learned some ways of getting out of our passivity and we need to pass it on to our kids, no matter how old they are. Observe your kids and see if you can identify where Satan is working passivity into their lives.

Who are your children?

Name	Age	Strengths	Fears	Where can you help them?

Are you leading others? Who?

Who are you being lead or taught by?

Where are areas of your own passivity that you can push in for your kids?

If you have older children, how did you initiate them into adulthood or how could you? Remember that it is never too late.

If your children are still young, what would it take to start the planning process of the initiation?

chapter fourteen

More Tools

If you are like me, you can never have enough tools in the tool bag to get the job done. Finding what works for you will be key in recovering your inner hero's abilities. Be creative as you work through this section.

From the book:

> We all have joy that we could get by following the desires that are written on our hearts, but Satan is the great thwarter. He wounds us and then uses our passivity against us, from entering the desires of our heart. Some people feel that longing for joy but succumb to their passivity and check out with an addiction or choose not to engage because there are too many obstacles in the way. Others have been so taken out that they have no clue anymore what the desires written on their heart even look like.

What are the passions that God has written on your heart?

Jim Snyder

What joys have been lost?

What obstacles are in your way of pursuing our desires?

What struggles do you have with your faith?

What are you trusting God for?

Why don't you think God will come through for you?

Where is God not coming through for you?

Are you asking the right questions?

What sins might be standing in the way of God coming through for you?

What lies does Satan get you to believe?

From the book:

> The idea of competition can send a passive man into a tailspin as it usually means conflict. There is a lot of risk involved in competition so many guys do not engage in it because of the outcomes. On the other hand, many people who engage in competition but allow passivity to dictate how far they progress in it and what areas are affected.

Where do you avoid competition?

Where do you embrace competition?

How can you more regularly embrace healthy competition?

What games do you play with your family and wife?

What fears come to mind when you think about joining organized sports?

What Do Dads do you use as reminders? What do they stand for?

Who can you trust with your goals?

What issues are you willing to risk telling others?

chapter fifteen

Where to Go From Here

Working through the book and this workbook was probably a great ordeal. Continue to find areas to push in, wounds that need to be healed, and areas that you can risk in. Just a few follow up questions for you.

What were the reasons you started reading the book?

Have they changed? How?

What does your momentum look like?

What would it look like if your passivity was a thing of the past?

What will your world look like when you are fully alive?

What does/did a day of passivity look like in your life? Document one.

What does a day of engagement look like in your life? Document one.

What is one small step you can work on today moving from your average passive day to your ideal engaged day?

So the question remains: where to go from here? This is a question that can only be answered by you as it is your life's story that you are writing, will it be one of winning the game or one of watching the game unfold. I can't wait to hear about your story.

Blessings, my brother, and remain encouraged (the infusion of courage through the act of forging with a hammer and anvil) in our Heavenly Father.

Your Brother in Christ,
Jim

About the Author

Jim Snyder is a follower of Christ, a husband to a wonderful wife, a father to some amazing kids, counselor to his clients, and ministry leader. He came to Christ late in his life after having spent most of his twenty-one years in the computer industry, including acquiring an advanced degree, before fully engaging in his calling as a counselor. Jim had been lay or peer counseling for a handful of years before God convicted him of becoming a full time professional counselor. In 2005, Jim went back to school at Colorado Christian University in Lakewood, Colorado, and received his Master's of Arts in counseling. His counseling ministry originally focused on helping men overcome sexual integrity issues but was altered after Jim attended a Wild at Heart boot camp put on by Ransomed Heart Ministries. He then began working with men who were struggling with any problems, including their sexual integrity and especially their passivity. Jim is a die-hard fly-fisherman and enjoys scuba diving whenever he gets the chance. He enjoys seeing men set free from Satan's matrix of lies and subsequently freedom for their families.